D1563557

# Neither Victims nor Executioners

# Neither Victims nor Executioners

*An Ethic Superior to Murder*

ALBERT CAMUS

*Translated by Dwight Macdonald*

*With a new introduction by*
*Peter Klotz-Chamberlin and Scott Kennedy*

Published in Commemoration of the Thirtieth Anniversary
of the Resource Center for Nonviolence,
Santa Cruz, California, www.rcnv.org

WIPF & STOCK · Eugene, Oregon

In association with the Resource Center for Nonviolence

Wipf and Stock Publishers
199 W 8th Ave, Suite 3
Eugene, OR 97401

Neither Victims nor Executioners, Second Edition
An Ethic Superior to Murder
By Camus, Albert
Copyright©1946 Gallimard
ISBN 13: 978-1-55635-771-8
Publication date 12/13/2007
Previously published by New Society Publishers, 1986

*For*

*Doug Rand*
*(April 4, 1952–March 5, 2000),*

*William Stringfellow*
*(April 26, 1928–March 2, 1985),*

*and*

*the Villagers of Ighil Hammad*

"Engagement in specific and incessant struggle
against death's rule renders us human. . . .
In resistance, persons live most humanly.
'No' to death means 'yes' to life."

—William Stringfellow,
*An Ethic for Christians and Other Aliens in a Strange Land*

# Contents

## Introduction: An Ethic Superior to Murder

The Resource Center for Nonviolence reprinted Albert Camus' *Neither Victims nor Executioners* more than two decades ago to commemorate the tenth anniversary of our founding in Santa Cruz, California, in 1976. We chose Camus' seminal essay because it speaks powerfully to the responsibility of the individual in a social contract that renders murder unacceptable, a core principle of nonviolence. When military action continues to lead American foreign policy, and war and terror dominate a new century, Camus' particular perspective on the possibility and necessity of resistance to violence has become even more important.

Camus' prescient 1946 essay asks that we consider the consequences of continuing to identify with age-old cultural justifications for violence.

- If indeed, as Camus writes, "there is no suffering, no torture anywhere in the world which does not affect our everyday lives," can we ignore the distant consequences of our actions and the reality of systemic forms of violence?

- Can we "defend" our society and its values with a "defense" establishment that erodes them and with weapons of mass destruction that, if used, will obliterate the very values and destroy the very society the weapons presume to secure?

- Does our preoccupation with national security and self-perceived national interests justify the dehumanization of others as "the enemy," as things that are somehow less human and deserving of life than ourselves?

- Do we in effect embrace violence in the vain hope of ridding the world of violence?

- What would it mean for murder to be no longer legitimated? If society refused to sanction the taking of human life for any reason, what would change in social institutions that today tolerate, or even rely on, ultimate resort to murder?

- What would constitute a genuine revolution today, one that would embody humankind's aspirations for freedom and justice and life itself without denying them to others?

- What would change in our lives, and in our participation in political and economic institutions, if we commit to a social contract that refuses to justify killing for any reason or cause or nation?

*Neither Victims nor Executioners* advocates the alternative of choosing new identities that would contribute to a "modest utopia," a new culture that does not dream of ending either evil or violence, but adopts a refusal to legitimize killing. It is this call to which the Resource Center for Nonviolence has sought to respond for more than three decades.

Two decades ago, the Soviet-American Super Power rivalry was the dominant dynamic in what Camus named "the century of fear." While that particularly threatening century has concluded, the question Camus pressed in 1946 remains at the forefront of our consciousness: "Who can deny that we live in a state of terror?" Since 9/11, obsession with terror has overtaken the U.S. government like fire in a dry forest. An especially powerful dynamic stoking that firestorm is popular participation in what Camus calls "obedience to abstractions," obedience that fuels fanaticism and terror in the United States as well as around the globe. People readily identify with words written by Albert Camus before many of us were born: "The most striking feature of the world we live in is that most of its inhabitants . . . are cut off from the future."

The dread of calamities has extended from the renewed threat of weapons of mass destruction in the hands of extra-state groups or nations, to threats from economic and technological attacks on the environment, catastrophic global warming, pollution of water and air, pandemic, or starvation. Albert Camus understood in 1946, "Instead of simply blaming everything on this fear, we should consider it as one of the basic factors in the situation, and try to do something about it. No task is more important."

Camus' essay, written immediately after World War II, straddled the years of war in Europe and the Pacific and the emerging Cold War. As a member of the French Resistance to the Nazis, Camus caught early glimpses of problems arising in the square off between the Soviet Bloc and the West led by the United States. His insights are as compelling and relevant today as the US succumbs to *hubris* and overreach as the world's sole Super Power, most tragically in Iraq.

Before Camus' essay and before World War II, many people in Europe and North America had already identified the problems of war. Utter disgust in response to the horrors of World War I prompted widespread support for pacifism during the 1930s. An Oxford Union resolution in England in 1933 had proclaimed that its signers would under no circumstances "fight for

King and country," attracting the support of tens of thousands of young men. In the US, the Pledge took on a different form as a refusal "to support the United States government in any war it may conduct." A few short years later, many of those signing the Oxford Pledge had already succumbed to the logic of fighting for a just cause by joining in or supporting the battle against fascism in Spain. This turnabout on support for violence represented a kind of political pacifism that was akin to being a vegetarian between meals. Most of the remaining pacifists and isolationists who opposed war eventually acquiesced to the necessity of armed force to triumph over fascism in Germany and its allied states. Pacifists offered no concerted resistance to the course of events that led to Hitler's aggression and made scant contribution to his eventual defeat.

As World War II heated up, anti-war activists found themselves reduced in numbers and increasingly marginalized. Pacifism faced internal collapse and external rejection because of its outdated and irresponsible isolationism. It too often failed to address the realities of international conflict and growing global interdependence. Pacifists displayed considerable heroism as individuals or small groups in resisting Nazism and the Holocaust in some dramatic instances, such as in Le Chambon Sur Lignon and a dozen other villages in Haute-Loire in southern France, which courageously provided refuge to and spirited thousands of Jews and others across the Alps to safety. With the defeat of Hitler and Hirohito, however, the pacifists' somewhat naive and sometimes unrealistic view of human nature could not withstand the horrific revelations of the Nazi death camps and the apparent success of the atomic bombings of Hiroshima and Nagasaki in bringing the war to an early end.

Camus recognized that World War II was for most people in the West the example *par excellence* of the just war. The rise of totalitarianism in Germany and Italy, the aggression of Imperial Japan and Nazi Germany against neighboring states, and the belated acknowledgment of Hitler's genocide against the Jews and others, however, all served for most people to justify whatever measures the Allies employed to overcome such monstrous evils, even embracing the United States' use of atomic weapons against Hiroshima and Nagasaki.

Still today, many pacifists see their disavowal of violence as a form of personal witness. Others advocate active nonviolence as a force for national defense, unseating dictatorial regimes, defending human rights, achieving social justice, and furthering social good. Just as pacifists were not able to adequately speak to fears of the public threatened by fascism, advocates of nonviolence are struggling to pose credible alternatives to national security ideology in the face of the real and imagined threats of global terrorism. McCarthyism in the 1950s and Bushism in the first decade of the third millennium rely significantly on widespread fear and insecurity. The populations of even the most powerful nations are susceptible to fear-driven manipulation by those wielding military power.

While World War II largely knocked the wind out of the pacifists' sails, Europeans reeled from the devastation that totalitarianism and war had wreaked on their society. Their cities were destroyed and their economies in shambles. Before the blood had dried on the soil, Europe was rent into two armed camps. The Soviets, confident that they had won the war at the cost of 22 million casualties, believed they had well earned their place as a global political and military heavyweight. The mutually exclusive, self-justifying ideologies of the West and the Russian-dominated East set the stage for what political and literary commentator Dwight Macdonald describes as a snowballing "decline to barbarism."

The US, meanwhile, enjoyed a hard-won victory, prosperity buoyed by a bloated defense economy, and new stature as the dominant world power. As a result, people in the United States have felt perfectly justified using whatever means necessary to defend freedom against tyranny. In the decades after World War II, this rule of thumb justified the use of sheer force—economic, political, and if need be, military, to preserve the US's perceived self-interests around the world and to protect "the American way of life." Foreign intervention became the norm for conducting American policy, with the US averaging a dozen military actions abroad each decade since 1945.

Geostrategists had already anticipated the Cold War in their military and political moves as World War II drew to a close. Gar Alperovitz (*The Decision to Use the Atomic Bomb*) and others have convincingly argued that the atomic bombing of Japan was not the final necessary blow of World War II but the first blow of the Cold War. Most people, of course, were appalled by the unprecedented violence of the war. Afterward, some even believed that creation of the United Nations and the unthinkable destructiveness of "the Bomb" would render war obsolete.

The Allied Victory, as surely as the rise of Nazism, nevertheless strengthened and extended the power of what Walter Wink later described as "the myth of redemptive violence":

> The belief that violence 'saves' is so successful because it doesn't seem to be mythic in the least. Violence simply appears to be the nature of things. It's what works. It seems inevitable, the last and, often, the first resort in conflicts. If a god is what you turn to when all else fails, violence certainly functions as a god. What people overlook, then, is the religious character of violence. It demands from its devotees an absolute obedience-unto-death.

This killing logic, the so-called "necessities of war," culminated both in the Nazi death camps and the devastation of major cities. With the end of the war, despite utter exhaustion and foreboding about the emerging Super Power rivalry, very few people realized that something fundamental had died and an ominous threshold had been crossed. No worldview would be adequate if it failed to take into account the reality of evil on the greatest scale and the human capacity for genocidal hatred—symbolized by Auschwitz, and humankind's capacity to use wholesale violence in the name of a just cause—symbolized by the bombings of Dresden, Tokyo, and especially Hiroshima and Nagasaki.

Thomas Merton was among those who had come to this realization. Facing military conscription in World War II, he doubted whether the Allies could emerge victorious without eventually stooping to Hitler's level and embracing the Nazis' barbarous methods. Allied obliteration bombing of German cities and the American destruction of Hiroshima and Nagasaki ("Auschwitz raining from the sky," wrote Merton from his Trappist monastery) confirmed his worst fears.

Political commentator and sometimes pacifist Dwight Macdonald also noticed the crossing of this ominous threshold. During World War II, while those who opposed the Allied war against Hitler were dismissed as "unrealistic," Macdonald insisted that "the problems . . . could not be solved by a military victory of either side," and "the triumph of the lesser evil would turn out to be merely the triumph of the greater evil in a different form, and that a choice between an Allied and a Nazi victory was a choice between being strangled or poisoned."

Within days of the atomic bombings of Hiroshima and Nagasaki, Macdonald wrote that the futility of war was manifest and the very concept of war eclipsed by the reality of modern warfare. He was deeply troubled by scientists who had created the bomb but disavowed any personal responsibility for its use or effect. He also rejected attempts to blame the German people as a whole for the crimes of Nazism. "Today the tendency is to think of peoples as responsible and individuals as irresponsible. The reversal of both these conceptions is the first condition of escaping the present decline to barbarism. A considerable portion of the atrocious acts of the Germans . . . were chargeable rather to war in general than to any special inhumanity of the Germans."

It is no wonder, then, that Dwight Macdonald chose to give greater hearing to the writings of Albert Camus. Camus was among those who, after 1945, discerned that humankind had entered a new moment and faced a different set of questions, whether or not we chose to acknowledge them. In 1947 Macdonald translated Camus' *Neither Victims nor Executioners* for publication in the July/August 1947 issue of his English-Language journal *Politics*. Camus seems to have known little about others who had renounced violence—such as French pacifist André Trocmé of Le Chambon Sur Lignon, even though Camus wrote *The Plague* in Le Chambon in 1942 while recuperating from illness, or even so well-known a figure as Gandhi. He offers no systematic explanation of nonviolence as a method of collective struggle. Nevertheless, Camus' adamant, articulate, and enduring essay ranks among the foremost renunciations of violence as a political method. As people and nations were drawing lines and taking sides, each fully confirmed in their worldview and reliance on force by the events of World War II, Albert Camus rebelled against the emerging polarity and its competing justifications of violence.

Anticipating the Cold War, Camus wrote, "Some of us feel too strongly our common humanity to make such a choice. Those who really love the Russian people . . . do not wish for them success in power-politics, but rather want to spare them, after the ordeals of the past, a new and even more terrible blood-letting. So, too, with the American people and with the peoples of unhappy Europe."

Camus saw the writing on the wall.

Without benefit of later revelations of Stalin's barbarous attacks on the Soviet people, Camus foresaw the dangerous excesses of blind obedience to Marxist ideology. As a result, he suffered alienation from many of his former Resistance comrades. In the heady aftermath of liberation, he also recognized the seeds of US intervention in Vietnam, Central America, Iraq, and elsewhere.

Camus' critique of modern warfare, ideology, and the irresponsibility of humankind in the modern era breaks with the centuries-old Just War tradition and its various secular echoes. He understood that traditional theoretical constraints on war, such as the inviolability of civilians and the principle of proportionality (that the presumed good to come out of a war must outweigh the destructiveness required to achieve it), were clearly superfluous in a total war such as World War II and nullified altogether by nuclear weaponry.

The Just War Doctrine sought to legitimate the taking of human life within clear constraints, to protect a supposedly divinely appointed government. But since at least World War II, the Just War Doctrine has been co-opted by the nation-state. "The state has become an end in itself," wrote Macdonald in 1943, "subjugating the human being as the Church did in the Middle Ages. In the new religion of the State . . . peoples of the world are being organized into vast power-states, military-socialist in form, which are devastating the globe in their internecine struggles."

The new Nation State arrogates to itself the prerogatives formerly enjoyed by the Church: demanding unquestioning loyalty, imposing orthodoxy, suppressing dissent, eroding personal conscience, and sanctifying violence. The trend, according to Camus, is "to give to Caesar those functions which formerly belonged to God."

The State reinforces divisions in the human community by defining its own interests as at odds with others. It further engenders irresponsibility by subordinating the individual citizen's conscience to the State's dictates.

Camus especially abhorred the State's role as an abstraction serving to legitimate murder, symbolized most clearly in the emerging ideology of the national security state, a staple of the political Right that also served to legitimize murder in the eyes of many of his Leftist colleagues. This ideology was simultaneously used to justify domestic repression and a resort to violence in foreign affairs. So far as Camus was concerned, neither the American West nor the Soviet East sufficiently embodied the positive values they espoused to justify their use or legitimization of murder. He once remarked, "No government is ever pure or wise enough to claim the power to kill." Camus suggested Europe would do well to disengage from the murderous polarity that emerged after the war.

While North Americans facilely identified totalitarian characteristics in the Soviet Union, the national security ideology more subtly but no less certainly permeated the US body politic. The United States in turn exported this ideology by training, funding, supporting, and defending various dictatorial regimes. In Latin America and the Middle East, for example, the use of surveillance and torture is endemic and the melding of police and armed forces into a single apparatus of control and repression systemic. Several such regimes that enjoy US support flagrantly and consistently disregard or violate the most fundamental human rights, universally recognized rights, which define the individual as distinct from the State. The state of permanent war declared by President Bush as an essential quality of the "War on Terror" after the 9/11 terrorist attacks has further reinforced the grip of the national security state ideology on the US. This is evidenced by erosion of fundamental rights in the Patriot Act and widespread human rights abuse and use of torture in Guantanamo and Abu Ghraib and through "extraordinary rendition."

The national security state is not simply a Republican Party or neo-conservative invention. Collective punishment reaching genocidal proportions preceded the war in Iraq. In 1996 following the First Gulf War, barely halfway through a dozen years of US-led and enforced economic sanctions against Iraq, humanitarian groups reported that the sanctions had caused the death of a half-million Iraqi children under five years of age. Madeleine Albright, Secretary of State for the Clinton Administration, brushed off such reports, "I think this is a very hard choice, but the price—we think the price is worth it."

On September 11, 2001, the US government again faced a choice. The US could investigate the sources of hatred that commandeered such heinous acts and work to constructively redress claims while seeking out the perpetrators of the monstrous crimes. The United States chose instead to return fear for fear and terror for terror, by declaring a "total war on terror," a war to continue until "evil is defeated." In answer to 2,800 deaths, the United States embraced responsibility for hundreds of thousands of deaths in Iraq and Afghanistan as well as loss and maiming of thousands of US combatants. The War on Terror is without end, confirming Camus' prediction that "Fear means . . . a world where murder is legitimate and where human life is considered trifling."

Thus, Camus apprehended Merton's troubled vision of the triumph of Hitler as evident in the prevalence of the national security state ideology in the Soviet Bloc, in the West, and in the Third World. The State compromises the values it is meant to defend and promote. It violates the very things that originally attracted the loyalty, commitment, and sacrifice of its citizenry.

Camus saw also the ominous role of technology in the national security state. Technology not only vastly increases the lethality of means of murder, but also further distances executioners from the consequences of their deeds. The Allied bomber squadrons obliterated square miles of German cities and returned to their officers' clubs to celebrate. Thousands of engineers design and produce weapons of mass destruction, such as the nuclear first strike Trident submarine, that then Seattle Archbishop Raymond Hunthausen described as "the Auschwitz of Puget Sound." US workers mass produce cluster bombs, designed to eviscerate human bodies, and their delivery is speeded up for widespread use by Israel in its periodic wars on Lebanon. This work is done in the comfort of air-conditioned offices, where weapons are tested, war games played, mega-deaths calculated at computer terminals, and victims seldom observed except in a fleeting television image.

The depersonalization of murder goes hand in hand with modern civilization's bureaucratic social organization. Individuals typically deny responsibility for the results of bureaucratic actions. Increasingly isolated individuals live as atomized strangers in a mass society. People are primarily identified as spectators and consumers of goods, news, and analyses. "Authorities" appeal to individual desires and fears rather than nurturing a common life and social interrelationships. Obedience to the national security state is valued over individual responsibility for the victims of social policy. When asked after 9/11 how the American people could support the War on Terror, Bush could only advise Americans to continue to shop.

In modern society it is not only possible to ignore the human consequences of military policies. It is in fact difficult to see and understand the human costs of modern warfare. In the devastation of Europe, Camus saw the material manifestation of a profoundly disturbing cultural event—the destruction of the human community by the rule of violence and murder. Just causes and righteous ideologies were defended by the highest expressions of reason and advanced by the most modern technology. To Albert Camus, such legitimization was nothing more than a facade masking fratricide.

The power of national security ideology rests in its shaping of political consciousness. It justifies state violence by obscuring the consequences of that violence to those who fall victim to it. The precedent of our nation's collective amnesia was already well established in the wake of World War II with our attitude toward the atomic bombings of Hiroshima and Nagasaki. As a nation, the US has also proven incapable of coming to grips with what our rich and powerful country did to the small country of Vietnam and its impoverished people. Though prevailing on the ground, Vietnam did not enjoy "the victor's justice," which was the prerogative of the Allies after World War II. There were no public war crime tribunals with high-ranking government officials or military officers in the dock, no formal pronouncements of national repentance, no follow through on commitment to reparations and assistance in reconstruction by the US government. Rather the US failed to make good on commitments made at the Paris Peace talks to help rebuild shattered Vietnam. More

13

than three decades later, the US still has not accepted responsibility for the long-term and devastating effects of widespread use of napalm and Agent Orange, even with our own veterans, not to mention the Vietnamese.

After Vietnam, the American people were again spared having to face the sobering reality of modern warfare, its nature, function, and consequence. President George H. W. Bush officially declared that the United States had been cured of the "Vietnam Syndrome" following the First Gulf War. The door was opened for his son, George W. Bush, to commit US ground forces in Afghanistan and to wage "preventive war" on Iraq. Now the lessons of US intervention in Vietnam are being painfully relearned in Iraq.

Camus demanded that the umbilical cord connecting the reality of violence with its moral justification be severed. He rejected politics that justify violence as "realistic." He insisted that there must be alternative courses of action for a world "cut off from the future" by enslavement to unremitting and redundant violence. He condemned developments that reduce people to mere abstractions and the individual to little more than a representative of an ideology. Camus asserted a personalism in which individuals are responsible for their actions in the world. He also maintained a cosmopolitanism that honors our human bond with others around the world, across national borders and transcending separations of any type.

*Neither Victims nor Executioners* doggedly points us to the tragic historical cycle in which victims of tyranny and violence employ violence in pursuit of a peaceful and just world. The issue for Camus is not a question of right intentions. All parties to conflict typically consider themselves motivated by just cause or self-defense. God's favor is always claimed by both sides of a conflict. The issue is the use of violence itself, the use of murder for presumably "just" causes in the illusory hope of eliminating murder.

Camus consistently uses the term "murder" to shock the reader into recognizing the personal consequences of all sorts of killing. By choice of the word "murder," he simply means the taking of human life in any form, including for a supposedly just cause or national purpose. Camus championed opposition to the death penalty, for example, and was an outspoken defender of human rights. He refused the moral certitude of those who accept murder and intimidation as necessary parts of their program, whether as ideologues, demagogues, patriots, revolutionaries, social engineers, or what he called "Servants of History."

The word "murder" strips away the impersonal language of war where killing becomes "collateral damage" or an abstract statistic. Murder is personal. When killing was executed in unprecedented genocidal scale by both sides in World War II, and threatened in even greater scale by emerging powers following the war, Camus insisted this killing was still personal for victim and for perpetrator. It was murder. In murder, there is a victim and there is a murderer—an executioner. When killing is experienced and understood personally, as murder, it poses a basic question that Camus contends every person must address. And he offers an answer that, if widely accepted, would turn the world's politics on its head.

Would we willingly consent to bearing the brunt of what another considers legitimate violence? If not, how can we rationalize the victimization of others with violence we consider perfectly legitimate? If we would not be victims, how can we consciously be executioners? No matter how strongly we are convinced or how positively motivated we may be, how can we rationalize the murder of others?

Camus would have us break the cycle of violence and its attendant legitimization. The direct, responsible, and human way to say "No!" to legitimizing murder is, according to Camus, to say no to being an executioner. Only then can we fairly say no to the possibility of being a victim. To refuse being a victim requires us to refuse being an executioner.

Renunciation of violence and murder is for Camus a moral imperative in its own right. But it was also the practical consequence of a basic social contract. Camus concludes that those who identify with the victims of injustice or oppression must recognize how their own political loyalties and beliefs legitimate murder. Quite simply, those who do not wish to be victims of murder must refuse to be executioners and refuse to view the taking of human life as legitimate.

This straightforward formula in effect shifts responsibility for the downward spiral of violence, with its increasing ferocity and lethality, from abstract forces beyond human control to the individual person. Camus' primary concern is, "What can we do?" While acknowledging that many of the forces of violence and catastrophe will go on with or without us, for Camus "the end of the world" is already present in a deadly culture. "We live in terror because persuasion is no longer possible . . . because we live in a world of abstractions, of bureaus and machines, of absolute ideas and of crude messianism. We suffocate among people who think they are absolutely right, whether in their machines or in their ideas. And for all who can live only in an atmosphere of human dialogue and sociability, this silence is the end of the world."

Because violence and murder, even in their grossest expressions, are perfectly legitimate in the eyes of those perpetrating the violence, Camus looks squarely at the consequences of such actions. He forces us to see the human face of those victimized

16

by violence. He then examines the motivating principles for this abhorrent destruction of human life. Whether the taking of life is perceived as an ideological imperative or as a necessary evil, the result for Camus is the same: it is still murder. Camus rejects murder because of its totally unacceptable consequence: the depersonalization and trivialization of human life.

In fact, few of us are personally confronted with the choice to murder or not. Technology places murder at a great distance even from those who are in the killing business. An open-ended war is waged against Iraq with little perceptible impact on daily life in the United States, but for those with loved ones serving or killed or injured in the fighting. Many justify their dismissal of the pacifist's conscientious refusal to accept the taking of human life by pointing to those who are deranged or evil and likely to kill. The other person would kill and therefore murder is necessary.

Camus differs from many pacifists in his disavowal of the possibility of eliminating murder altogether. He considers such a goal utopian—beyond or outside of human experience. For Camus, it is, rather, the justification or rationalization of killing that must cease.

People will kill because they can do nothing else, whether from lack of perceived alternatives or the crush of circumstances. However, as the French Protestant theologian and former member of the Resistance movement Jacques Ellul argues, even such taking of human life must not be rationalized as though it could ever enjoy God's blessing. It is wrong, cannot be legitimate, and must be rejected per se. Camus writes, "If there are many today who, in their secret hearts, detest violence and killing, there are not many who care to recognize that this forces them to reconsider their actions and thoughts." The issues he raises strike at the very heart of how we understand ourselves and the means by which we seek to express our deepest commitments.

Camus insists that we all look at the part we play in murder, however far removed. He reasserts the primacy of personal responsibility in place of ideology, technology, warfare, and murder in the daily fabric of modern life. He especially rejects violence sanctioned by that relatively new abstraction, the Nation State, with its high level of organization, its reliance on the technology of the police-state and modern warfare, its fervent standard bearing for ethnocentrism, nationalism, and self-interest, and its service in the name of redemptive violence.

Obsessive nationalism, conviction of racial superiority, religious chauvinism, defense of material interests, and the economies that sustain them all depend on the exercise of police force or military power. They rest on the foundation of a preparedness to kill. When we look at the fact of murderous violence in the world, Camus insists that the choice we must make is not whether or not we kill, but whether or not we justify killing. Do we legitimate murder?

And, Camus emphasizes, this question touches each one of us. If we doubt the future of our world due to violence, we need ask ourselves: Do we support or allow the killing of any people for any reason? Do we accept and support institutions that employ killing in the conduct of their policies? Do groups that enjoy our loyalty, material support, commitment, and acceptance defend the use of violence and lethal force?

Camus' challenge is not only to those who embrace violence as part of their political method. To those who recognize a "common humanity" and personally forego recourse to violent means, Camus declares that "good will" is not enough. In addition to a refusal to kill, vigorous action must be taken to delegitimize the institutions and depersonalizing actions of systemic injustice, national security state ideologies, and technologies, which combine to trivialize the human person.

*Neither Victims nor Executioners* sets a human course in defiance of the "decline to barbarism" of which Macdonald warned. Camus sought above all to reaffirm the responsibility of individuals. And he sought to restore a human face to a world run amok with depersonalized violence. Anticipating the "nuclear pacifism" of Thomas Merton and others two decades later, Camus' essay also presaged the emerging consensus in several churches in Europe and North America in the 1980s that war and deterrence based on Mutual Assured Destruction are morally indefensible. And his argument buttresses the growing secular movements around the globe that apprehend the urgency of abolishing war and recognizing worldwide interrelatedness.

In place of the wholesale irresponsibility evidenced by all sides during World War II, and those lining up with West or East in its aftermath, Camus sets forth an active cultivation of human respect, a restoration of dialogue, greater conviviality, and authentic diversity.

Though Camus cannot be considered a conventional pacifist, there is a remarkable confluence between his perspective and that of Gandhi. Camus identifies a fundamental symbiosis between ends and means. Ends may justify means, but not, according to both Camus and Gandhi, any and every means, especially murder.

Camus' *Neither Victims nor Executioners* excels in naming and spelling out the grounds for rejecting the social reality of modern violence. It addresses the personal consequence (being the victim of murder), and reaffirms the personal responsibility (choosing to be an executioner).

But, in the end, his essay is as provocative for what is left unsaid as for what is said.

Camus' proposals for action overvalue the isolated individual's responsibility. He relies almost entirely on "dialogue" and the use of persuasion through the exchange of ideas. His ultimate solution is some ill-defined world government in which reason will prevail. He did not have benefit of observing the United Nations struggling to reach its potential or fulfill its mandate. Camus' response is understandable given the factors shaping his writing: the author's isolation from radical nonviolent social movements addressing fundamental injustice while disavowing violence, the optimism arising from the founding of the United Nations, and Camus' own intellectual capacities and gift of speech. But further dimensions of a response to the reality and futility of violence must be examined.

The problem of violence is so pervasive in modern society that it needs a forceful, well-organized, and collective response as well. Since Camus' essay was written, the power of nonviolence, not only as a force for personal transformation but also as a method of social change, has been more clearly demonstrated. Gandhi's national liberation movement, the Iranian people's overthrow of the Shah, the Polish workers' obstruction of the armed might of the Soviet Union, the forced abdication of Ferdinand Marcos as President of the Philippines, the dissolution of the Soviet Union by rebelling Eastern European nations, and the first Palestinian uprising, all attest to the power of people acting in concert to resist oppression and defend human life.

New insights are being gleaned about the power of nonviolence from so many quarters—from unarmed accompaniment projects defending human rights workers and communities threatened by violence to experiments with Peace Villages in Colombia and nonviolence villages in Palestine, to mass popular protest in Myanmar/Burma and the Ukraine. Yet when Camus, Gandhi, Martin Luther King, Jeannette Rankin, Phil Berrigan,

Cesar Chavez, Dorothy Day, or Kathy Kelly reflect further on the refusal to participate indirectly with killing, they understand such a choice is not a comforting moral conclusion, not simply affiliating with a different political party. The choice means a change of one's role in society and of one's identity. Camus says, "Let us suppose that certain individuals resolve that they will consistently oppose to power the force of example; to authority, exhortation; to insult, friend reasoning; to trickery, simple honor. Let us suppose they refuse all the advantages of present-day society and accept only the duties and obligations which bind them to other [people]." And, "There is no idea of constructing a new ideology, but rather of discovering a style of life."

We must refute the simplistic choices so often presented in politics: support nation-state militarism or violent revolution, capitalism or communism, electoral politics or political irrelevancy, this way or that. We must seek a third way, an alternative to armed camps, a method of waging conflict and engaging in social struggle that refuses to legitimize or advocate anyone's domination or murder. Political strategies must be devised that enable us to change social, political, and economic structures. Militant, though unarmed, examples of social struggle abound worldwide. But these strategies must nurture a change in attitudes and values at the same time as they pursue political objectives.

Camus calls to those of us "who are not of any party—or [who are] ill at ease in the party we have chosen," who are "without a kingdom," who renounce politics that justify killing for any reason—for the victims, for democracy, for justice, for peace, for civilizations—we who live in "anguish" over the knowledge of our contradictory predicament as victims and executioners, we who want to be neither: "I think it would be better . . . to try to understand and clarify this anguish, see what it means, interpret

21

its quasi-total rejection of a world which provokes it, and trace out the feeble hope that suffuses it."

The Hebrew prophet wrote, "I put before you life and death; therefore choose life." Choosing life in all sorts of circumstances is what gives people of all cultures meaning. When lives are at risk, acute awareness of victims, of our own vulnerability, of oppression and damage to others, is fundamental to the human person. Service and defense of victims is our highest calling.

World War II saw the advent of weapons of mass destruction, which literally foreshadowed the end of the world. That war also revealed the extent to which society has been enthralled by resort to murderous means to perpetrate evil—and in the vain hope of destroying evil. Six decades later, people's sense of being "closed to the future" is more pervasive than perhaps ever before. This deep-seated and well-founded fear has become a part of who we are. The bomb that Camus so feared in the hands of the United States has now spread to many others. The national security state of Hitler's dream now spans the political spectrum from left to right. Humankind has witnessed qualitative and quantitative leaps in its capacity to commit murder.

Still, the question remains: Are we capable of rising to an ethic superior to murder?

In the end, Camus' challenge is one of imagination. Can we truly imagine another person's death or our own shared responsibility for it? Can we see ourselves as perpetrators of violence as well as its potential victims? Can we recognize another person, another culture, another ideology as worthy of coexistence instead of ultimate defeat by our way? Can we imagine that other people's children are as precious as our own?

Forming an answer to these questions begins with recognition of our common humanity. We must find the answers together, even with those against whom we struggle.

If we are to restore hope in our common future, Albert Camus urges us to commit to a new social contract. Our politics and our personal ways of life must begin with a refusal to kill, with an unwillingness to accept others as deserving victims for any reason or allegiance.

It is time for each of us to distinguish ourselves from many around us in disavowing any sanction to violence and any legitimacy to murder.

—Peter Klotz-Chamberlin
and Scott Kennedy
Easter 1986
Revised October 2007
kenncruz@pacbell.net

# Neither Victims nor Executioners

*Albert Camus*

# The Century of Fear

The 17th century was the century of mathematics, the 18th that of the physical sciences, and the 19th that of biology. Our 20th century is the century of fear. I will be told that fear is not a science. But science must be somewhat involved since its latest theoretical advances have brought it to the point of negating itself while its perfected technology threatens the globe itself with destruction. Moreover, although fear itself cannot be considered a science, it is certainly a technique.

The most striking feature of the world we live in is that most of its inhabitants—with the exception of pietists of various kinds—are cut off from the future. Life has no validity unless it can project itself toward the future, can ripen and progress. Living against a wall is a dog's life. True—and the men of my generation, those who are going into the factories and the colleges, have lived and are living more and more like dogs.

This is not the first time, of course, that men have confronted a future materially closed to them. But hitherto they have been able to transcend the dilemma by words, by protests, by appealing to other values which lent them hope. Today no one speaks any more (except those who repeat themselves) because history seems to be in the grip of blind and deaf forces which will heed neither cries of warning, nor advice, nor entreaties. The years we have gone through have killed something in us. And that something is simply the old confidence man had in himself, which led him to believe that he could always elicit human reactions from another man if he spoke to him in the language of a common humanity. We have seen men lie, degrade, kill, deport, torture—and each time it was not possible to persuade them not to do these things because they were sure of themselves and because one cannot appeal to an abstraction, i.e., the representative of an ideology.

Mankind's long dialogue has just come to an end. And naturally a man with whom one cannot reason is a man to be feared. The result is that—besides those who have not spoken out because they thought it useless—a vast conspiracy of silence has spread all about us, a conspiracy accepted by those who are frightened and who rationalize their fears in order to hide them from themselves, a conspiracy fostered by those whose interest it is to do so. "You shouldn't talk about the Russian culture purge—it helps reaction." "Don't mention the Anglo-American support of Franco—it encourages Communism." Fear is certainly a technique.

What with the general fear of a war now being prepared by all nations and the specific fear of murderous ideologies, who can deny that we live in a state of terror? We live in terror because persuasion is no longer possible; because man has been wholly submerged in History; because he can no longer tap that part of his nature, as real as the historical part, which he recaptures in contemplating the beauty of nature and of human faces; because we live in a world of abstractions, of bureaus and machines, of absolute ideas and of crude messianism. We suffocate among people who think they are absolutely right, whether in their machines or in their ideas. And for all who can live only in an atmosphere of human dialogue and sociability, this silence is the end of the world.

To emerge from this terror, we must be able to reflect and to act accordingly. But an atmosphere of terror hardly encourages reflection. I believe, however, that instead of simply blaming everything on this fear, we should consider it as one of the basic factors in the situation, and try to do something about it. No task is more important. For it involves the fate of a considerable number of Europeans who, fed up with the lies and violence, deceived in their dearest hopes and repelled by the idea of killing their fellow men in order to convince them, likewise repudiate the idea of themselves being convinced that way. And yet such is the alternative that at present confronts so many of us in Europe who are not of any party—or ill at ease in the party we have chosen—who doubt socialism has been realized in Russia or liberalism in America, who grant to each side the right to affirm its truth but refuse it the right to impose it by murder, individual or collective. Among the powerful of today, these are the men without a kingdom. Their viewpoint will not be recognized (and I say "recognized," not "triumph"), nor will they recover their kingdom until they come to know precisely what they want and proclaim it directly and boldly enough to make their words a stimulus to action. And if an atmosphere of fear does not encourage accurate thinking, then they must first of all come to terms with fear.

To come to terms, one must understand what fear means: what it implies and what it rejects. It implies and rejects the same fact: a world where murder is legitimate, and where human life is considered trifling. This is the great political question of our times, and before dealing with other issues, one must take a position on it. Before anything can be done, two questions must be put: "Do you or do you not, directly or indirectly, want to be killed or assaulted? Do you or do you not, directly or indirectly, want to kill or assault?" All who say No to both these questions are automatically committed to a series of consequences which must modify their way of posing the problem. My aim here is to clarify two or three of these consequences.

## Saving Our Skins

I once said that, after the experiences of the last two years, I could no longer hold to any truth which might oblige me, directly or indirectly, to demand a man's life. Certain friends whom I respected retorted that I was living in Utopia, that there was no political truth which could not one day reduce us to such an extremity, and that we must therefore either run the risk of this extremity or else simply put up with the world as it is.

They argued the point most forcefully. But I think they were able to put such force into it only because they were unable to really *imagine* other people's death. It is a freak of the times. We make love by telephone, we work not on matter but on machines, and we kill and are killed by proxy. We gain in cleanliness, but lose in understanding.

But the argument has another, indirect meaning: it poses the question of Utopia. People like myself want not a world in which murder no longer exists (we are not so crazy as that!) but rather one in which murder is not legitimate. Here indeed we are Utopian—and contradictory. For we do live, it is true, in a world where murder is legitimate, and we ought to change it if we do not like it. But it appears that we cannot change it without risking murder. Murder thus throws us back on murder, and we will continue to live in terror whether we accept the fact

31

with resignation or wish to abolish it by means which merely replace one terror with another.

It seems to me every one should think this over. For what strikes me, in the midst of polemics, threats and outbursts of violence, is the fundamental good will of every one. From Right to Left, every one, with the exception of a few swindlers, believes that his particular truth is the one to make men happy. And yet the combination of all these good intentions has produced the present infernal world, where men are killed, threatened and deported, where war is prepared; where one cannot speak freely without being insulted or betrayed. Thus if people like ourselves live in a state of contradiction, we are not the only ones, and those who accuse us of Utopianism are possibly themselves also living in a Utopia, a different one but perhaps a more costly one in the end.

Let us, then, admit that our refusal to legitimize murder forces us to reconsider our whole idea of Utopia. This much seems clear: Utopia is whatever is in contradiction with reality. From this standpoint, it would be completely Utopian to wish that men should no longer kill each other. That would be absolute Utopia. But a much sounder Utopia is that which insists that murder be no longer legitimized. Indeed, the Marxian and the capitalist ideologies, both based on the idea of progress, both certain that the application of their principles must inevitably bring about a harmonious society, are Utopian to a much greater degree. Furthermore, they are both at the moment costing us dearly.

We may therefore conclude, practically, that in the next few years the struggle will be not between the forces of Utopia and the forces of reality, but between different Utopias which are attempting to be born into reality. It will be simply a matter of choosing the least costly among them. I am convinced that we can no longer reasonably hope to save everything, but that we can at least propose to save our skins, so that *a* future, if not *the* future, remains a possibility.

Thus (1) to refuse to sanction murder is no more Utopian than the "realistic" ideologies of our day, and (2) the whole point is whether these latter are more or less costly. It may, therefore, be useful to try to define, in Utopian terms, the conditions which are needed to bring about the pacification of men and nations. This line of thought, assuming it is carried on without fear and without pretensions, may help to create the preconditions for clear thinking and a provisional agreement between men who want to be neither victims nor executioners. In what follows, the attempt will be not to work out a complete position, but simply to correct some current misconceptions and to pose the question of Utopia as accurately as possible. The attempt, in short, will be to define the conditions for a political position that is modest— i.e., free of messianism and disencumbered of nostalgia for an earthly paradise.

## The Self-Deception of the Socialists

If we agree that we have lived for ten years in a state of terror and still so live, and that this terror is our chief source of anxiety, then we must see what we can oppose to this terror. Which brings up the question of socialism. For terror is legitimized only if we assent to the principle: "the end justifies the means." And this principle in turn may be accepted only if the effectiveness of an action is posed as an absolute end, as in nihilistic ideologies (anything goes, success is the only thing worth talking about), or in those philosophies which make History an absolute end (Hegel, followed by Marx: the end being a classless society, everything is good that leads to it).

Such is the problem confronting French Socialists, for example. They are bothered by scruples. Violence and oppression, of which they had hitherto only a theoretical idea, they have now seen at first hand. And they have had to ask themselves whether, as their philosophy requires, they would consent to use that violence themselves, even as a temporary expedient and for a quite different end. The author of a recent preface to Saint-Just, speaking of men of an earlier age who had similar scruples, wrote contemptuously: "They recoiled in the face of horrors." True enough. And so they deserved to be despised by strong, superior spirits who could live among horrors without flinching. But all the same, they gave a voice to the agonized appeal of commonplace spirits like ourselves,

34

the millions who constitute the raw material of History and must someday be taken into account, despite all contempt.

A more important task, I think, is to try to understand the state of contradiction and confusion in which our Socialists now exist. We have not thought enough about the moral crisis of French Socialism, as expressed, for example, in a recent party congress. It is clear that our Socialists, under the influence of Léon Blum and even more under the pressure of events, have preoccupied themselves much more with moral questions (the end does not justify all means) than in the past. Quite properly, they wanted to base themselves on principles which rise superior to murder. It is also clear that these same Socialists want to preserve Marxian doctrine, some because they think one cannot be revolutionary without being Marxist, others, by fidelity to party tradition, which tells them that one cannot be socialist without being Marxist. The chief task of the last party congress was to reconcile the desire for a morality superior to murder with the determination to remain faithful to Marxism. But one cannot reconcile what is irreconcilable.

For if it is clear that Marxism is true and there is logic in History, then political realism is legitimate. It is equally clear that if the moral values extolled by the Socialist Party are legitimate, then Marxism is absolutely false since it claims to be absolutely true. From this point of view, the famous "going beyond" Marxism in an idealistic and humanitarian direction is a joke and an idle dream. It is impossible to "go beyond" Marx, for he himself carried his thought to its extreme logical consequences. The Communists have a solid logical basis for using the lies and the violence which the Socialists reject, and the basis is that very dialectic which the Socialists want to preserve. It is therefore hardly surprising that the Socialist congress ended by simply putting forward simultaneously two contradictory positions—a conclusion whose sterility appears in the results of the recent elections.

This way, confusion will never end. A choice was necessary, and the Socialists would not or could not choose.

I have chosen this example not to score off the Socialists but to illustrate the paradoxes among which we live. To score off the Socialists, one would have to be superior to them. This is not yet the case. On the contrary, I think this contradiction is common to all those of whom I speak, those who want a society which we can both enjoy and respect; those who want men to be both free and just, but who hesitate between a freedom in which they know justice is finally betrayed and a justice in which they see freedom suppressed from the first. Those who know What Is To Be Done or What Is To Be Thought make fun of this intolerable anguish. But I think it would be better, instead of jeering at it, to try to understand and clarify this anguish, see what it means, interpret its quasi-total rejection of a world which provokes it, and trace out the feeble hope that suffuses it.

A hope that is grounded precisely in this contradiction, since it forces—or will force—the Socialists to make a choice. They will either admit that the end justifies the means, in which case murder can be legitimized; or else, they will reject Marxism as an absolute philosophy, confining themselves to its critical aspect, which is often valuable. If they choose the first, their moral crisis will be ended, and their position will be unambiguous. If the second, they will exemplify the way our period marks the end of ideologies, that is, of absolute Utopias which destroy themselves, in History, by the price they ultimately exact. It will then be necessary to choose a more modest and less costly Utopia. At least it is in these terms that the refusal to legitimize murder forces us to pose the problem.

Yes, that is the question we must put, and no one, I think, will venture to answer it lightly.

## Parody of Revolution

Since August 1944, everybody talks about revolution, and quite sincerely too. But sincerity is not in itself a virtue: some kinds are so confused that they are worse than lies. Not the language of the heart but merely that of clear thinking is what we need today. Ideally, a revolution is a change in political and economic institutions in order to introduce more freedom and justice; practically, it is a complex of historical events, often undesirable ones, which brings about the happy transformation.

Can one say that we use this word today in its classical sense? When people nowadays hear the word "revolution," they think of a change in property relations (generally collectivization) which may be brought about either by majority legislation or by a minority coup.

This concept obviously lacks meaning in present historical circumstances. For one thing, the violent seizure of power is a romantic idea which the perfection of armaments has made illusory. Since the repressive apparatus of a modern State commands tanks and airplanes, tanks and airplanes are needed to counter it. 1789 and 1917 are still historic dates, but they are no longer historic examples.

And even assuming this conquest of power were possible, by violence or by law, it would be effective only if France (or Italy or Czechoslovakia) could be put into parentheses and isolated from the rest of the world. For, in the actual historical situation of 1946, a change in our own property system would involve, to give only one example, such consequences to our American credits that our economy would be threatened with ruin. A right-wing coup would be no more successful, because of Russia with her millions of French Communist voters and her position as the dominant continental power. The truth is— excuse me for stating openly what every one knows and no one says—the truth is that we French are not free to make a revolution. Or at least that we can be no longer revolutionary all by ourselves, since there no longer exists any policy, conservative or socialist, which can operate exclusively within a national framework.

Thus we can only speak of world revolution. The revolution will be made on a world scale or it will not be made at all. But what meaning does this expression still retain? There was a time when it was thought that international reform would be brought about by the conjunction or the synchronization of a number of national revolutions—a kind of totting-up of miracles. But today one can conceive only the extension of a revolution that has already succeeded. This is something Stalin has very well understood, and it is the kindest explanation of his policies (the other being to refuse Russia the right to speak in the name of revolution).

This viewpoint boils down to conceiving of Europe and the West as a single nation in which a powerful and well-armed minority is struggling to take power.

But if the conservative forces—in this case the USA—are equally well armed, clearly the idea of revolution is replaced by that of ideological warfare. More precisely, world revolution today involves a very great danger of war. Every future revolution will be a foreign revolution. It will begin with a military occupation—or, what comes to the same thing, the blackmail threat of one. And it will become significant only when the occupying power has conquered the rest of the world.

Inside national boundaries, revolutions have already been costly enough—a cost that has been accepted because of the progress they are assumed to bring. Today the cost of a world war must be weighed against the progress that may be hoped for from either Russia or America gaining world power. And I think it of first importance that such a balance be struck, and that for once we use a little imagination about what this globe, where already thirty million fresh corpses lie, will be like after a cataclysm which will cost us ten times as many.

Note that this is a truly objective approach, taking account only of reality without bringing in ideological or sentimental considerations. It should give pause to those who talk lightly of revolution. The *present-day* content of this word must be accepted or rejected as a whole. If it be accepted, then one must recognize a conscious responsibility for the coming war. If rejected, then one must either come out for the status quo—which is a mood of absolute Utopia insofar as it assumes the "freezing" of history—or else give a new content to the word "revolution," which means assenting to what might be called relative Utopia. Those who want to change the world must, it seems to me, now choose between the charnel house threatened by the impossible dream of history suddenly struck motionless, and the acceptance of a relative Utopia which gives some leeway to action and to mankind. Relative Utopia is the only realistic choice; it is our last frail hope of saving our skins.

# International Democracy and Dictatorship

We know today that there are no more islands, that frontiers are just lines on a map. We know that in a steadily accelerating world, where the Atlantic is crossed in less than a day and Moscow speaks to Washington in a few minutes, we are forced into fraternity—or complicity. The forties have taught us that an injury done a student in Prague strikes down simultaneously a worker in Clichy, that blood shed on the banks of a Central European river brings a Texas farmer to spill his own blood in the Ardennes, which he sees for the first time. There is no suffering, no torture anywhere in the world which does not affect our everyday lives.

Many Americans would like to go on living closed off in their own society, which they find good. Many Russians perhaps would like to carry on their Statist experiment holding aloof from the capitalist world. They cannot do so, nor will they ever again be able to do so. Likewise, no economic problem, however minor it appears, can be solved outside the comity of nations. Europe's bread is in Buenos Aires. Siberian machine-tools are made in Detroit. Today, tragedy is collective.

We know, then, without a shadow of a doubt, that the new order we seek cannot be merely national, or even continental; certainly not occidental nor oriental. It must be universal. No longer can we hope for anything from partial solutions or concessions. We are living in a state of compromise, i.e, anguish today and murder tomorrow. And all the while the pace of history and the world is accelerating. The 21 deaf men, the war criminals of tomorrow who today negotiate the peace, carry on their monotonous conversations placidly seated in an express train which bears them toward the abyss at a thousand miles an hour.

What are the methods by which this world unity may be achieved, this international revolution realized in which the resources of men, of raw materials, of commercial markets and cultural riches may be better distributed? I see only two, and these two between them define our ultimate alternative.

The world can be united from above, by a single State more powerful than the others. The USSR or the USA could do it. I have nothing to say to the claim that they could rule and remodel the world in the image of their own society. As a Frenchman, and still more as a Mediterranean, I find the idea repellent. But I do not insist on this sentimental argument. My only objection is, as stated in the last section, that this unification could not be accomplished without war—or at least without serious risk of war. I will even grant what I do not believe: that it would not be an atomic war. The fact remains, nevertheless, that the coming war will leave humanity so mutilated and impoverished that the very idea of law and order will become anachronistic. Marx could justify, as he did, the war of 1870, for it was a provincial war fought with Chassepot rifles. In the Marxian perspective, a

43

hundred thousand corpses are nothing if they are the price of the happiness of hundreds of millions of men. But the sure death of millions of men for the hypothetical happiness of the survivors seems too high a price to pay. The dizzy rate at which weapons have evolved, a historical fact ignored by Marx, forces us to raise anew the whole question of means and ends. And in this instance, the means can leave us little doubt about the end. Whatever the desired end, however lofty and necessary, whether happiness or justice or liberty—the means employed to attain it represent so enormous a risk and are so disproportionate to the slender hopes of success, that, in all sober objectivity, we must refuse to run this risk.

This leaves us only the alternative method of achieving a world order: the mutual agreement of all parties.

This agreement has a name: international democracy. Of course every one talks about the U.N. But what is international democracy? It is a democracy which is international. (The truism will perhaps be excused, since the most self-evident truths are also the ones most frequently distorted.) International— or national—democracy is a form of society in which law has authority over those governed, law being the expression of the common will as expressed in a legislative body. An international legal code is indeed now being prepared. But this code is made and broken by governments, that is by the executive power. We are thus faced with a regime of international dictatorship. The only way of extricating ourselves is to create a world parliament through elections in which all peoples will participate, which will enact legislation which will exercise authority over national governments. Since we do not have such a parliament, all we can do now is to resist international dictatorship; to resist on a world scale; and to resist by means which are not in contradiction with the end we seek.

## The World Speeds Up

As every one knows, political thought today lags more and more behind events. Thus the French fought the 1914 war with 1870 methods, and the 1939 war with 1918 methods. Antiquated thinking is not, however, a French specialty. We need only recall that the future of the world is being shaped by liberal-capitalist principles, developed in the 18th century and by "scientific socialist" principles developed in the 19th. Systems of thought which, in the former case, date from the early years of modern industrialism, and, in the latter, from the age of Darwinism and of Renanian optimism, now propose to master the age of the atomic bomb, of sudden mutations, and of nihilism.

It is true that consciousness is always lagging behind reality: History rushes onward while thought reflects. But this inevitable backwardness becomes more pronounced the faster History speeds up. The world has changed more in the past fifty years than it did in the previous two hundred years. Thus we see nations quarreling over frontiers when everyone knows that today frontiers are mere abstractions. Nationalism was, to all appearances, the dominant note at the Conference of the 21.

Today we concentrate our political thinking on the German problem, which is a secondary problem compared to the clash of empires which threatens us. But if tomorrow we resolve the Russo-American conflict, we may see ourselves once more outdistanced. Already the clash of empires is in process of becoming secondary to the clash of civilizations. Everywhere the colonial peoples are asserting themselves. Perhaps in ten years, perhaps in fifty, the dominance of Western civilization itself will be called into question. We might as well recognize this now, and admit these civilizations into the world parliament, so that its code of law may become truly universal, and a universal order be established.

The veto issue in the U.N. today is a false issue because the conflicting majorities and minorities are false. The USSR will always have the right to reject majority rule so long as it is a majority of ministers and not a majority of peoples, all peoples, represented by their delegates. Once such a majority comes into being, then each nation must obey it or else reject its law—that is, openly proclaim its will to dominate....

To reply once more and finally to the accusation of Utopia: for us, the choice is simple, Utopia or the war now being prepared by antiquated modes of thought.... Skeptical though we are (and as I am), realism forces us to this Utopian alternative. When our Utopia has become part of history, as with many others of like kind, men will find themselves unable to conceive reality without it. For History is simply man's desperate effort to give body to his most clairvoyant dreams.

## A New Social Contract

All contemporary political thinking which refuses to justify lies and murder is led to the following conclusions: (1) domestic policy is in itself a secondary matter; (2) the only problem is the creation of a world order which will bring about those lasting reforms which are the distinguishing mark of a revolution; (3) within any given nation there exist now only administrative problems, to be solved provisionally after a fashion, until a solution is worked out which will be more effective because more general.

For example, the French Constitution can only be evaluated in terms of the support it gives or fails to give to a world order based on justice and the free exchange of ideas. From this viewpoint, we must criticize the indifference of our Constitution to the simplest human liberties. And we must also recognize that the problem of restoring the food supply is ten times more important than such issues as nationalization or election figures. Nationalization will not work in a single country. And although the food supply cannot be assured either within a single country, it is a more pressing problem and calls for expedients, provisional though they may be.

And so this viewpoint gives us a hitherto lacking criterion by which to judge domestic policy. Thirty editorials in *Aube* may range themselves every month against thirty in *Humanité*, but they will not cause us to forget that both newspapers, together with the parties they represent, have acquiesced in the annexation without a referendum of Briga and Tenda, and that they are thus accomplices in the destruction of international democracy. Regardless of their good or bad intentions, Mr. Bidault and Mr. Thorez are both in favor of international dictatorship. From this aspect, whatever other opinion one may have of them, they represent in our politics not realism but the most disastrous kind of Utopianism.

Yes, we must minimize domestic politics. A crisis which tears the whole world apart must be met on a world scale. A social system for everybody which will somewhat allay each one's misery and fear is today our logical objective. But that calls for action and for sacrifices, that is, for men. And if there are many today who, in their secret hearts, detest violence and killing, there are not many who care to recognize that this forces them to reconsider their actions and thoughts. Those who want to make such an effort, however, will find in such a social system a rational hope and a guide to action.

They will admit that little is to be expected from present-day governments, since these live and act according to a murderous code. Hope remains only in the most difficult task of all: to reconsider everything from the ground up, so as to shape a living society inside a dying society. Men must therefore, as individuals, draw up among themselves, within frontiers and across them, a new social contract which will unite them according to more reasonable principles.

The peace movement I speak of could base itself, inside nations, on work-communities and, internationally, on intellectual communities; the former, organized cooperatively, would help as many individuals as possible to solve their material problems, while the latter would try to define the values by which this international community would live, and would also plead its cause on every occasion.

More precisely, the latter's task would be to speak out clearly against the confusions of the Terror and at the same time to define the values by which a peaceful world may live. The first objectives might be the drawing up of an international code of justice whose Article No. 1 would be the abolition of the death penalty, and an exposition of the basic principles of a sociable culture (*"civilisation du dialogue"*). Such an undertaking would answer the needs of an era which has found no philosophical justification for that thirst for fraternity which today burns in Western man. There is no idea, naturally, of constructing a new ideology, but rather of discovering a style of life.

Let us suppose that certain individuals resolve that they will consistently oppose to power the force of example; to authority, exhortation; to insult, friendly reasoning; to trickery, simple honor. Let us suppose they refuse all the advantages of present-day society and accept only the duties and obligations which bind them to other men. Let us suppose they devote themselves to orienting education, the press and public opinion toward the principles outlined here. Then I say that such men would be acting not as

Utopians but as honest realists. They would be preparing the future and at the same time knocking down a few of the walls which imprison us today. If realism be the art of taking into account both the present and the future, of gaining the most while sacrificing the least, then who can fail to see the positively dazzling realism of such behavior?

Whether these men will arise or not I do not know. It is probable that most of them are even now thinking things over, and that is good. But one thing is sure: their efforts will be effective only to the degree they have the courage to give up, for the present, some of their dreams, so as to grasp the more firmly the essential point on which our very lives depend. Once there, it will perhaps turn out to be necessary, before they are done, to raise their voices.

## Towards Sociability

Yes, we must raise our voices. Up to this point, I have refrained from appealing to emotion. We are being torn apart by a logic of History which we have elaborated in every detail—a net which threatens to strangle us. It is not emotion which can cut through the web of a logic which has gone to irrational lengths, but only reason which can meet logic on its own ground. But I should not want to leave the impression, in concluding, that any program for the future can get along without our powers of love and indignation. I am well aware that it takes a powerful prime mover to get men into motion and that it is hard to throw one's self into a struggle whose objectives are so modest and where hope has only a rational basis—and hardly even that. But the problem is not how to carry men away; it is essential, on the contrary, that they not be carried away but rather that they be made to understand clearly what they are doing.

To save what can be saved so as to open up some kind of future—that is the prime mover, the passion and the sacrifice that is required. It demands only that we reflect and then decide, clearly, whether humanity's lot must be made still more miserable in order to achieve far-off and shadowy ends, whether we should accept a world bristling with arms where brother kills brother; or whether, on the contrary, we should avoid bloodshed and misery as much as possible so that we give a chance for survival to later generations better equipped than we are.

For my part, I am fairly sure that I have made the choice. And, having chosen, I think that I must speak out, that I must state that I will never again be one of those, whoever they be, who compromise with murder, and that I must take the consequences of such a decision. The thing is done, and that is as far as I can go at present. Before concluding, however, I want to make clear the spirit in which this article is written.

We are asked to love or to hate such and such a country and such and such a people. But some of us feel too strongly our common humanity to make such a choice. Those who really love the Russian people, in gratitude for what they have never ceased to be— that world leaven which Tolstoy and Gorky speak of—do not wish for them success in power-politics, but rather want to spare them, after the ordeals of the past, a new and even more terrible bloodletting. So, too, with the American people, and with the peoples of unhappy Europe. This is the kind of elementary truth we are liable to forget amidst the furious passions of our time.

Yes, it is fear and silence and the spiritual isolation they cause that must be fought today. And it is sociability (*"le dialogue"*) and the universal intercommunication of men that must be defended. Slavery, injustice and lies destroy this intercourse and forbid this sociability; and so we must reject them.

But these evils are today the very stuff of History, so that many consider them necessary evils. It is true that we cannot "escape History," since we are in it up to our necks. But one may propose to fight within History to preserve from History that part of man which is not its proper province. That is all I have tried to say here. The "point" of this article may be summed up as follows:

Modern nations are driven by powerful forces along the roads of power and domination. I will not say that these forces should be furthered or that they should be obstructed. They hardly need our help and, for the moment, they laugh at attempts to hinder them. They will, then, continue. But I will ask only this simple question: What if these forces wind up in a dead end, what if that logic of History on which so many now rely turns out to be a will o' the wisp? What if, despite two or three world wars, despite the sacrifice of several generations and a whole system of values, our grandchildren—supposing they survive—find themselves no closer to a world society? It may well be that the survivors of such an experience will be too weak to understand their own sufferings. Since these forces are working themselves out and since it is inevitable that they continue to do so, there is no reason why some of us should not take on the job of keeping alive, through the apocalyptic historical vista that stretches before us, a modest thoughtfulness which, without pretending to solve everything, will constantly be prepared to give some human meaning to everyday life. The essential thing is that people should carefully weigh the price they must pay.

To conclude: All I ask is that, in the midst of a murderous world, we agree to reflect on murder and to make a choice. After that, we can distinguish those who accept the consequences of being murderers themselves or the accomplices of murderers, and those who refuse to do so with all their force and being. Since this terrible dividing line does actually exist, it will be a gain if it be clearly marked. Over the expanse of five continents throughout the coming years an endless struggle is going to be pursued between violence and friendly persuasion, a struggle in which, granted, the former has a thousand times the chances of success than that of the latter. But I have always held that, if he who bases his hopes on human nature is a fool, he who gives up in the face of circumstances is a coward. And henceforth, the only honorable course will be to stake everything on a formidable gamble: that words are more powerful than munitions.

*Translated by Dwight Macdonald*

# Postscript

## FROM LE CHAMBON, TO ORADOUR AND IGHIL HAMMAD

During the summer of 2007, I visited Le Chambon-sur-Lignon. Le Chambon is one of a dozen villages in southern France that saved an estimated five thousand people fleeing the Nazis, including 3,500 Jews and many children. Thousands of children were integrated into boarding houses, hidden in homes, provided refuge in surrounding forests, or adopted into families. *Yad Vashem*, the Holocaust Martyrs' and Heroes' Remembrance Authority in Israel, honored Le Chambon as the first town to be recognized among the "Righteous Gentiles" who risked or gave their lives saving Jews during the Holocaust.

Le Chambon is a French Protestant village with a history of dissent and tight-knit community. Many years later, however, interviews with those rescued revealed that the people who participated in the widespread rescue effort during World War II included those from all walks of life, farmers and merchants and every profession, different faith communities and those with secular worldviews, and people of every age. There were no reports of any villager reporting on their neighbors' activities to the Nazis or their French collaborators.

Hanne Hirsch-Liebmann, whose life was saved, stated simply, "If today we are not bitter like most survivors are, it is only due to the fact that we met people like Trocmé, Theis, Mrs. Philip, and the people of Le Chambon who simply showed us that life could be different. They were people who believed we must all live together and even risk our lives for our fellow beings." One commentator seized on Hannah Arendt's famous description of the "banality of evil" during the Nazi-era, remarking that the people of Le Chambon and the surrounding area simply practiced the "banality of goodness."

On the same trip, I also visited Oradour-sur-Glâne, a village that commemorates the horrors of the Nazi occupation of France.

During the final year of the war in Europe, French Resistance fighters escalated attacks on German occupying forces. A German officer reportedly was captured by Resistance forces in Oradour and threatened with public execution. An SS Panzer Division was sent to take hostages for a prison exchange. Instead, early on the morning of June 10, 1944, German forces sealed off the town. They locked the women and children in the church and set it on fire, shooting those who tried to escape. Male villagers were peremptorily executed. One hundred ninety men, 247 women, and 205 children were killed. The German forces looted the village and then razed it. In war crimes trials following the war and into the 1980s, former German officers defended their acts as necessary measures against "terrorists."

After the war, French President Charles de Gaulle announced that Oradour-sur-Glâne would not be rebuilt. The town was preserved instead as it had been left by the Nazis. Oradour remains today as a stark memorial to the cruelty of Nazi occupation and, according to some, a symbol of the suffering caused by war.

Rahim Chouane, an Algerian living in France, accompanied my wife Kris, daughter Megan, and me to both Le Chambon and Oradour. Rahim remarked that his Algerian education had provided little information about the Holocaust and even less about the French Resistance to the Nazi occupation. He had never heard of either Le Chambon or Oradour.

At one point, I referred to the simple sign at the entrance to Oradour. The sign consisted of two words, "*SOUVIENS-TOI*," with the English translation below: "REMEMBER." As we turned to go back to our car, Rahim observed with not a little irony that France apparently had not "remembered" Oradour fifteen years later. We asked him to explain.

Algeria at the time was considered fully part of France—at least by the French. The Algerians fought for freedom and called their uprising their "War of Independence." It was "the Algerian War" to the French. As anti-war student activists during the US war on Vietnam, we knew it as "the Algerian Revolution" and read Frantz Fanon's "The Wretched of the Earth."

Algeria's anti-colonial war ran for eight years, from 1954 to 1962. Algerian guerrilla warfare and French efforts to retain their colonial settler control of the North African country both relied on violence and terrorism against civilians, including the use of torture. There were a million Algerian casualties and the homes of nearly two million Algerians were destroyed before Algeria finally won its independence.

In 1958, according to Rahim's grandparents, a French forest guard was killed, presumably by the Algerian *Mujahadeen* or guerilla fighters. The killing took place near their village *Ighil Hammad* in the Maillot region of "Great *Kabylie*," the Northeastern '*Berber*' mountains of Algeria. As an act of revenge and part of its campaign of "pacification," the French army proceeded to kill thirteen villagers and razed *Ighil Hammad*. The French declared the site forbidden for civilians. The entire population was relocated to what the survivors called "the concentration camp" of *Saharidj*, where they and their descendants still live today. (I described to Rahim how American forces destroyed Vietnamese villages and created "strategic hamlets" in the futile colonial war that we inherited from the French in Indochina.) Several times each year, families still visit their former homes and olive trees.

Nations regularly exhort others to remember the atrocities that they have suffered. They declare that such suffering will happen "Never Again!"

Too often, however, history demonstrates that the next or the very same generation will employ the same murderous means to the same predictable ends. Victims become executioners, victimhood justifies execution. Executioners portray themselves as victims.

Thousands of French school children visit Oradour, the "Martyrs Village," each year. The nearby town has a well-developed tourist center and museum. Yet the heroic resistance of Le Chambon and villages like it are relatively unknown. Of course we should not forget or erase the memories of victimhood. But we must also uphold the memories of heroes that affirm humanity and nonviolence. Le Chambon-sur-Lignon is an example of people who responded directly to their victimization through military occupation with deep humanity and risk, without violence, and by offering a more inspiring memory than simply tragedy. They embodied service in the face of awful inhumanity.

Visits to Le Chambon-sur-Lignon and Oradour-sur-Glâne vividly reminded me of Camus' message that those who would not be victims must also and adamantly refuse to be executioners. This fundamental change of course is necessary if the human race is to get beyond the seemingly endless cycle of victim and executioner. The history of humanity and suffering of war might be better told by upholding those heroes of Le Chambon, who refused to be either victims or executioners. This message is tragically too little understood. It is a message that we must carry to Moscow, Beijing, Tel Aviv, Algiers, and Washington.

And it is a message that we must inscribe in our own hearts.

—Scott Kennedy
24 October 2007
United Nations Day

## About the Resource Center for Nonviolence

Located in Santa Cruz, California, the Resource Center for Nonviolence offers a variety of formats in which to explore the meaning and significance of nonviolence and the prospects for nonviolence in shaping our daily lives and work for social change.

The Resource Center provides settings for both structured and informal discussion and learning in many dimensions of nonviolence, including an internship program of a month or longer, weekend workshops, two-week nonviolence trainings for organizers, study groups, and summer workcamps. The staff is available to speak and to lead discussions or workshops. Individuals especially knowledgeable or with extraordinary experiences in nonviolence are occasionally invited to Santa Cruz as residents. The Center also has a large library on Gandhi and nonviolence, a literature service and books for sale, and a periodic newsletter.

www.rcnv.org

Peter Klotz-Chamberlin and Scott Kennedy were among the co-founders of the Resource Center for Nonviolence. Peter Klotz-Chamberlin currently chairs the Center's Steering Committee. Scott Kennedy is Coordinator of the Center's Middle East Program and General Nonviolence Program.